My First Book about Sharks

Amazing Animal Books Children's Picture Books

By Molly Davidson

Mendon Cottage Books

JD-Biz Publishing

Read More Amazing Animal Books

Purchase at Amazon.com

Download Free Books!
http://MendonCottageBooks.com

Table of Contents

Introduction to Sharks

In an aquarium, sharks are one of the most requested fish to be seen, by visitors.

There are two types of sharks, those that live in salt water, like the ocean, and those that live in fresh water.

Many sharks are big and scary, but not all of them.

Shark Catfish

This type of catfish has a catlike head, with a skinny body.

Shark Catfish in the St. Petersburg Aquarium
<u>Wikimedia Commons</u>

It is very calm, and it is known to eat a lot.

Shark catfish can survive in fresh or salt water.

Shark catfish like to be in large groups.

Iridescent Shark Catfish

Wikimedia Commons

The Red Tailed Shark

This shark likes to live in a tube, a cave, or a pipe.

Red tails can grow to be 5 inches long and swim in schools with at least 6 others.

Red Tailed Black Shark

Wikimedia Commons

Rainbow Shark

Rainbow sharks are cranky, so they don't like to be with too many other fish.

They grow to about 9 inches in length.

Bala Shark

This type of shark is pretty happy and is usually hyper.

They are silver in color, with black lined fins and tail.

Bala shark like to travel in large groups.

Balantiocheilos Melanopterus (Bala Shark)

Wikimedia Commons

Great White Shark

Great white sharks have about 3,000 teeth which are in many rows.

Their favorite food is fish, but they also eat sea lions and seals.

The belly of a great white shark is white and their backs are gray.

They are adults when they have lived for more than 9 years.

They are usually about 15 feet long; the biggest ones are 21 feet long.

Great white sharks live in the ocean, by the coast where the water is warm.

Sharks are very curious, so to discover something new, they bite it, this is how humans get bit sometimes.

Bull Shark

They live on the Atlantic coast in the United States starting from Massachusetts in the north to Mexico.

Bull sharks like shallow water, so they will sometimes live in fresh water, like a river or bay.

They are about 11 1/2 feet long.

They are an adult when they turn 6 years old, they usually live to be about 14 years old.

A Carcharhinus Leucas (Bull Shark) in Playa Del Carmen, Mexico <u>Wikimedia Commons</u>

If a bull shark looses when of their strong teeth, they will just grow a new one.

They have very good hearing, and can sense water movement from a long ways away; this helps them hunt for food.

Bull sharks are the most dangerous sharks in the World, because they are very aggressive.

Bull sharks eat birds, bony fish, dolphins, other small sharks, and even other bull sharks.

A captured bull shark on the deck of a ship

Wikimedia Commons

Many humans are hunting bull sharks to make a Chinese dish called shark fin soup.

Tiger Shark

Tiger sharks are the fourth biggest shark in the whole world.

They can grow very big and long; an adult tiger shark can be 20 to 25 feet long, and can weigh up to 2,000 pounds.

A Tiger Shark in the Bahamas

Wikimedia Commons

When tiger sharks are young, they have strips like a tiger, but when they become an adult they go away.

They live in warm waters close to the shore.

Tiger sharks are very dangerous to people, they will attack, and then continue attacking until they know the person is dead.

Their jaws are so strong and their teeth are so sharp, they can crack open a sea turtle's shell with one bite.

Tiger Shark and Giant Trevelly fish in Maui, Hawaii's tropical waters

They are not an adult for about 12 to 18 years.

Hammerhead Shark

There are 9 species of the hammered shark; the biggest can weigh up to 500 pounds.

Hammerheads live from 20 to 30 years.

They do not lay eggs; the mother carries her babies (called pups) inside.

A mother hammerhead will give birth to 12 to 15 pups, then they are left to grow up on their own, the parents do not help them.

The eyes of a hammerhead are on the side of their head, so they can see above and below themselves at all times, which is helpful in hunting for food.

They hunt by themselves at night, and travel in large groups during the day.

Whale Shark

A whale shark is a very gentle animal; it will even let humans swim around it.

A whale shark is the largest fish in the whole ocean!

They live in all the oceans at one point in the year, they migrate through them all.

Its favorite food is fish and different small creatures found in the sea.

A whale shark can live up to 100 years.

Shark Attacks

Every year there are about 50 to 70 shark attacks all over the world.

The tiger, great white, and bull sharks are the main attackers of humans.

On the other hand, humans are killing 20 to 100 million sharks a year, because sharks get caught in fishing hooks or nets.

Shark Behavior

The skeleton of a shark is made of cartilage, what human noses are made of, while the skeleton of other fish are of bones.

Sharks breathe through 6 or 7 gill slits on their sides.

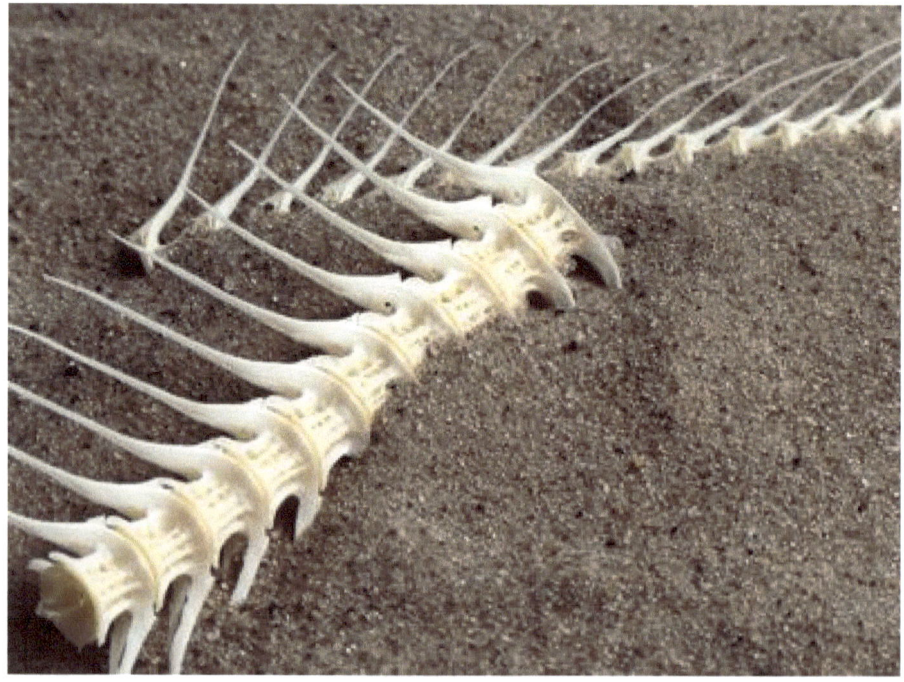

Shark Skeleton © ia_64 - Fotolia.com

Sharks can smell their prey from over a mile away!

Sharks can hear very low sounds, many that humans cannot even hear.

A shark's behavior depends on the time of day, the temperature, and the season.

Sharks will dive deeper in the summer then they will in the winter, because the deep water is colder in the winter.

What Sharks Look Like

Sharks have a large fin on their backs; it is called a dorsal fin.

They have a heart like we do, that pumps blood to every part of their body.

The tail fin is called a Caudal Fin, and this is what moves them forward, and steers them.

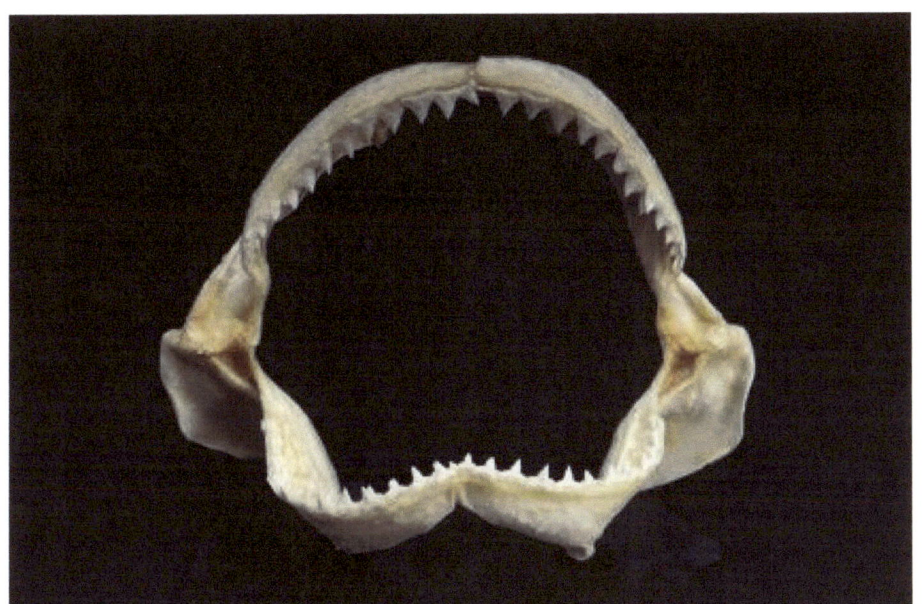

Shark Jaws © josephblake - Fotolia.com

Sharks have sharp teeth that are the shape of a triangle.

Facts about Sharks

The World's fastest shark is the Shortfin Mako, it can swim as fast as 20 miles per hour.

The deep water dogfish shark is the smallest salt water shark species and it has a length of about eight inches.

Blue sharks migrate from the North Atlantic Ocean, 3,740 miles to Brazil.

They will take breaks and rest, but sharks never sleep.

One last fact, sharks lived on the earth 200 million years before the dinosaurs did.

This is a Megalodon Shark, which was over 67 feet long, and became extinct with the dinosaurs.

Read More Amazing Animal Books

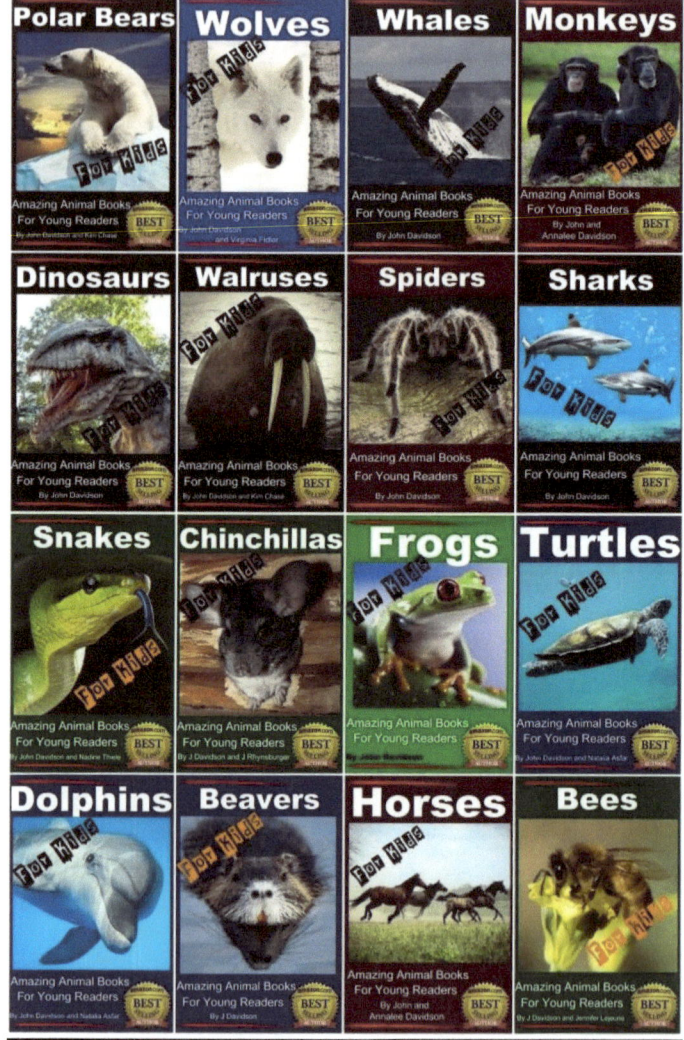

Purchase at Amazon.com

Download Free Books!
http://MendonCottageBooks.com

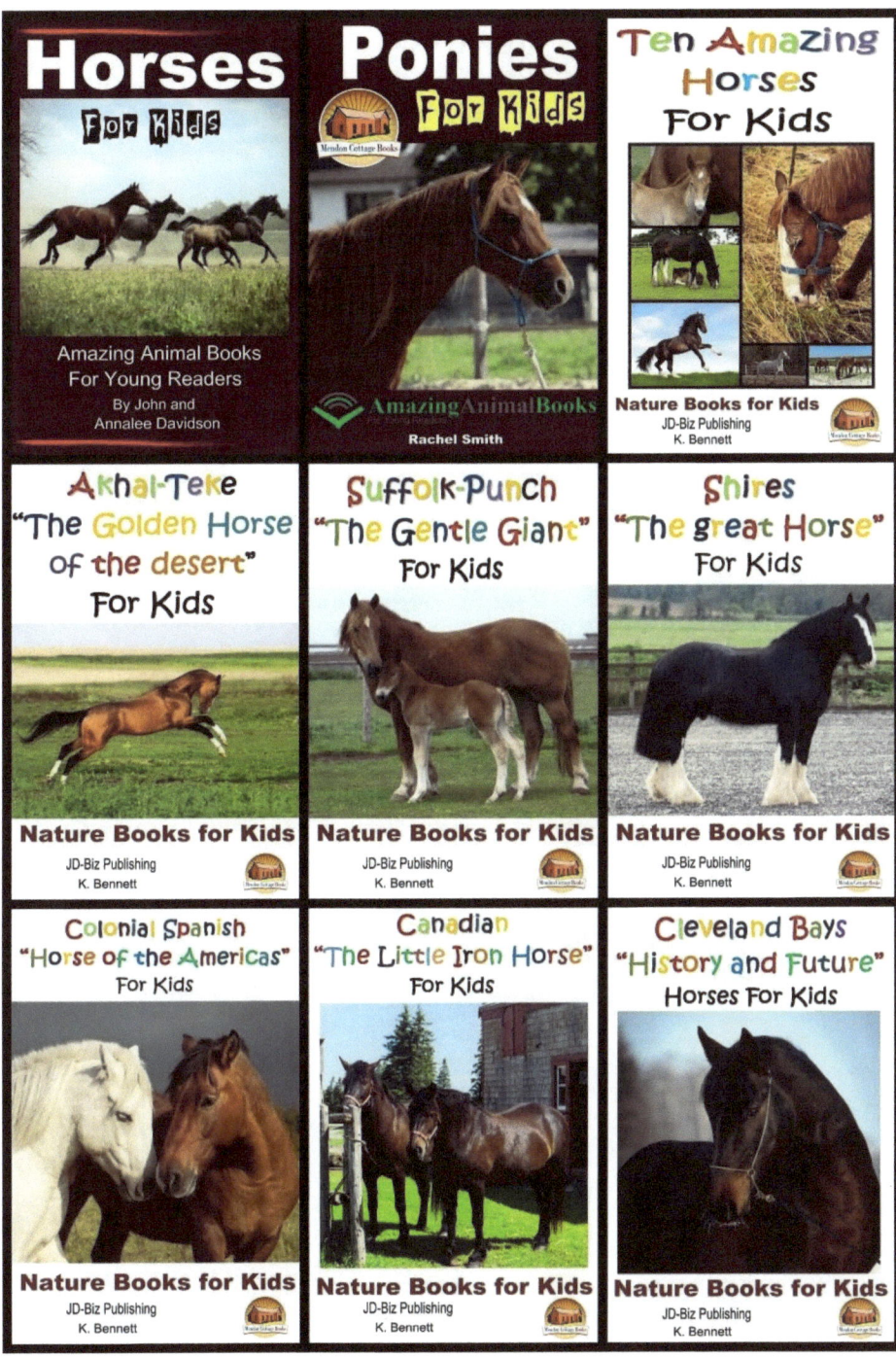

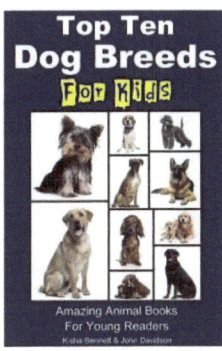

Top Ten Dog Breeds For Kids
Amazing Animal Books For Young Readers
Kisha Bennett & John Davidson

German Shepherds
Dog Books for Kids
K. Bennett

Bulldogs
Dog Books for Kids
K. Bennett

Dachshund
Dog Books for Kids
K. Bennett

Poodles
Dog Books for Kids
K. Bennett

Labrador Retrievers
Dog Books for Kids
K. Bennett

Rottweilers
Dog Books for Kids
K. Bennett

Boxers
Dog Books for Kids
K. Bennett

Golden Retrievers
Dog Books for Kids
K. Bennett

Puppies
Dog Books For Kids
Amazing Animal Books
By John Davidson

Beagles
Dog Books for Kids
K. Bennett

Yorkshire Terriers
Dog Books for Kids
K. Bennett

Dogs
Top Ten Dog Breeds For Kids
Amazing Animal Books For Young Readers
Zahra Jazeel & John Davidson

Cats For Kids
Amazing Animal Books For Young Readers
K. Bennett & John Davidson

Foxes For Kids
Amazing Animal Books For Young Readers
Zahra Jazeel & John Davidson

Wolves For Kids
Amazing Animal Books For Young Readers
By John Davidson and Virginia Fidler

Our books are available at

1. Amazon.com
2. Barnes and Noble
3. Itunes
4. Kobo
5. Smashwords
6. Google Play Books

Download Free Books!
http://MendonCottageBooks.com

Publisher

JD-Biz Corp

P O Box 374

Mendon, Utah 84325

http://www.jd-biz.com/

Mendon Cottage Books

P O Box 374, Mendon Utah 84325